COW

THE SCRAP MAN

in...

Raintree is an imprint of Capstone Global Library Limited, a company incorporated in England and Wales having its registered office at 7 Pilgrim Street, London, EC4V 6LB – Registered company number: 6695582

www.raintree.co.uk
myorders@raintree.co.uk

Designed by Hilary Wacholz
Edited by Sean Tulien
Original illustrations © Capstone 2016
Illustrated by Omar Lozano

ISBN 978 1 4747 1030 5 (paperback)
20 19 18 17 16
10 9 8 7 6 5 4 3 2 1

British Library Cataloguing in Publication Data: a full catalogue record for this book is available from the British Library.

Printed and bound in China.

FAR OUT FAIRY TALES

JAK
AND THE MAGIC
NANO-BEANS

A GRAPHIC NOVEL

BY CARL BOWEN

ILLUSTRATED BY OMAR LOZANO

Once upon a time, our people built an elevator that stretched all the way up to space.

Everybody who could afford the cost of the trip rode up and away to live among the clouds.

We never saw them again. They left the rest of us behind. Now everything's starting to break down. Soon we'll be surrounded by useless junk.

Just then, Mum called. Her avatar popped up on my wrist-phone.

Sheesh, Mum - I said I'd call you.

Right. But have you found him yet?

I did, I did. Relax, Mum.

Good girl. Wait right there. I'll send the scrap man your coordinates.

Sweetie, it's Mum. Have you found Cow yet?

BLEEP! BLEEP!

But you said I could take him back to the dealership!

Sweetie, that CDW-12 is worth more as parts. We'd never get anyone to buy the rusty robot he's become.

So do as I say and wait there until the scrap man shows up.

Whatever.

CLICK

15

Sheesh. Barely got that door closed in time.

TING!

Anyway, it's gone. If that giant doesn't burn up in the atmosphere, it'll wish it had when it crashes into Earth.

JAK... WE HAVE A PROBLEM.

What's wrong?

C'mon, Cow. Up and at 'em!

I CAN'T MOVE MY LEGS.

Oh, Cow...

I CAN'T USE MY THRUSTERS. AND WE HAVEN'T FOUND ANY NANOBOTS. I DON'T THINK WE CAN GET HOME NOW.

So much for helping our people...

LDW 12

The original version of *Jack and the Beanstalk* doesn't have a space elevator – but it *does* have a magic beanstalk that grows up into the sky!

Jack and his mother are very poor, so his mother tells him to go to the market and sell their cow. On the way there, Jack meets a mysterious stranger. The man offers to trade the cow for some "magic beans". Jack agrees, plants the beans in the ground and then brags to his mother about what he has done.

Jack's mother is furious with him for being tricked, and sends him to bed without supper. But when Jack wakes up the next day, he discovers a huge beanstalk growing all the way up into the clouds!

Jack leaps out of his window and climbs the beanstalk. When he reaches the clouds he finds a huge house and a giant woman! He begs the giant for some food, and she eventually agrees, but warns him to stay hidden from her husband. When the giant smells Jack, he cries out "Fee-fi-fo-fum, I smell the blood of an Englishman. Be he alive, or be he dead, I'll grind his bones to make my bread!" Jack stays hidden until the giant falls asleep.

Over time, Jack manages to steal two bags of gold and a golden hen from the giant. But when Jack tries to steal a golden harp, it calls out to the giant, waking him. The giant chases Jack out of the house and down the beanstalk. When Jack reaches the ground, he chops down the beanstalk with an axe before the giant can catch up. The giant falls to the ground and dies on impact.

With the two bags of gold, the hen and the harp, Jack and his mother live rich and happy lives together from that day on.

A **FAR OUT** GUIDE TO THE TALE'S SCI-FI TWISTS!

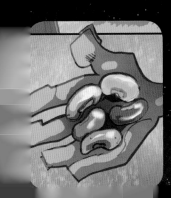

In the original story, Jack is a young boy. In this version, "Jak" is a young girl!

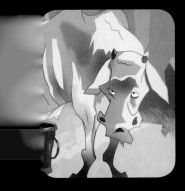

Milky-white, the cow from the fairy tale, is replaced by CDW-12, a robot called Cow.

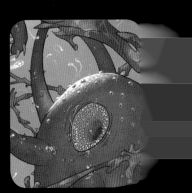

While a giant man tried to eat Jack in the fairy tale, Jak gets attacked by an octopus-like space monster!

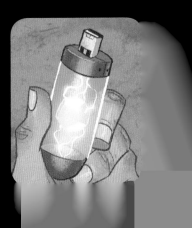

And the magic beans from the original tale have become tiny robots that fix up Jak's robotic friend, CDW-12!

VISUAL QUESTIONS

TING!

And we can help our planet!

TING!

TING!

Eww! What is that?

Little Bub only says one word throughout the entire book: "Ting". How is it using the word differently? What do you think it's saying in the panels?

What is going on in this scene (on page 22)? What is making the "gong" noises? Why did all the little fellas turn red (except for little Bub)?

GONG

Why, nothing but a *favour*...

I'm listening...

Who is the scrap man? Do you think he is trying to help Jak, their people or just himself? Why?

4

Jak called her family's CDW-12 robot "Cow". Why do you think she chose that nickname? In what ways is Cow like a normal cow? How is it different?

5

Who is telling the story in these narration boxes? Who is "our people" referring to? What planet do you think Jak is from? Do we know for sure?

Once upon a time, our people built an elevator that stretched all the way up to space.

Everybody who could afford the cost of the trip rode up and away to live among the clouds.

We never saw them again. They left the rest of us behind. Now everything's starting to break down. Soon we'll be surrounded by useless junk.

AUTHOR

Carl Bowen is a writer, husband and father living in Georgia, USA. He has written several comic books for children, including retellings of *20,000 Leagues Under the Sea* (by Jules Verne), *The Strange Case of Dr Jekyll and Mr Hyde* (by Robert Louis Stevenson), *The Jungle Book* (by Rudyard Kipling), "Aladdin and His Wonderful Lamp" (from A Thousand and One Nights), *Julius Caesar* (by William Shakespeare), and *The Murders in the Rue Morgue* (by Edgar Allan Poe). Carl's military fiction series of books called Shadow Squadron earned a star from Kirkus Book Reviews.

ILLUSTRATOR

Omar Lozano lives in Monterrey, Mexico. He has always been crazy about illustration and is constantly on the lookout for awesome things to draw. In his free time, he watches lots of films, reads fantasy and sci-fi books and draws! Omar has worked for Marvel, DC, IDW, Capstone and several other publishing companies.

GLOSSARY

airlock airtight chamber with a controlled level of air pressure that provides (or prevents) access to a space with a different air pressure (such as from inside a space station to outer space)

atmosphere mass of gases that surround a planet or star

avatar small picture that represents a computer user in a game, on the internet, etc. The picture does not have to look very much (or at all) like the user.

marvels things that are amazing, wonderful or extremely good

nanobots tiny, microscopic robots that some scientists believe will one day be able to replicate (create copies of themselves) in order to fix, repair or upgrade technology

scrap leftover, small piece of something after the main parts have been used. Scrapyards (places where scrap is left) often contain metal parts from vehicles, robots and other forms of technology.

surrounded moved close to someone or something on all sides in order to stop someone or something from escaping

swarm very large number of things moving together as one, like a swarm of bees (or nanobots!)

useless broken, or not producing or able to produce the effect you want